Boise State University Western Writers Series   Number 124

Richard Ronan

By Jan VanStavern

WITHDRAWN

Editors: James H. Maguire
John P. O'Grady

Business Manager:
James E. Hadden

Cover Design by Arny Skov

Cover autograph from the
Richard Ronan collection.
Used by permission of his
estate.

Boise State University, Boise, Idaho

Library of Congress Card No. 96-84301

International Standard Book No. 0-88430-123-0

Printed in the United States of America by
Boise State University Printing and Graphic Services
Boise, Idaho

Richard Ronan

Dedication

To my Mother,
Sue VanStavern,
For her own poetics of being.

Richard Ronan

The new world, the new times, the new peoples,
the new vistas, need a tongue according . . .
—Walt Whitman

I. INTRODUCTION

Richard Louis Ronan was a poet, playwright, and ikebana flower designer who lived in San Francisco with his partner, Bill Pittman, during the 1980s. He died of AIDS in 1989 at age 43, having produced six collections of poetry, seven plays, and several unpublished manuscripts. He received not only a Dodge Foundation Grant to teach poetry but also, while studying at Berkeley, the Emily Cook and Eisner Prizes. His versatility did not prevent him from excelling in several poetic forms: he wrote one of the strongest collections of narrative poetry published this half of the century, and the tension of his warring Zen and Catholic sensibilities gave life to an extraordinary lyric-dramatic poetry of the body.

His work as a gay poet imagining America and the West marks Ronan as a member of the "new brood" of poets Walt Whitman predicted in *Leaves of Grass*. Ronan experimented with direct and indirect techniques for writing about desire and homosexuality, the body and his country, using descriptive lists and many-gendered voices, to rise squarely to the challenge that "poets to come" carry Whitman's poetic beginnings forward, forging a writer's America.

Ronan's work, like his life, reflects the splits and doubling of a miscast, elegant man whose gay identity and Zen interests sometimes played dissonantly against his East Coast, Irish Catholic and German background. From his volumes published by Gay Sunshine Press to the pages of the mainstream *American Poetry Review*, Ronan's work plays out dramas of self and self-seeking. He reinterprets religion and the body in an attempt to give us a vision of the world marked by honest sexuality and evasive self-portrayal. His story unfolds across two time zones and spans three major fascinations: from East coast to West coast, through crosshatches of homosexual desire, Zen Buddhism, and his efforts to combine the visual and dramatic arts. Ronan's emotionally immediate, biographically elusive poetry closely follows these cuts and casts of his life. The work, as Lucien Stryk says in his preface to Ronan's *A Lamp of Small Sorrow* (1979), "tells the story of a spirit encountering its absolute context."

For the first thirty years of his life, Ronan was an ambivalent native of the eastern United States. In expressing his own erotic desire, his poetry reinterprets the myth of Western migration. In so doing, this reinterpretation establishes him not only as an important West Coast writer but also as a writer whose poetry shows many facets of what westering can mean, how the myth of the American West can matter to a gay poet from New Jersey.

This introduction to Ronan's poetic achievement will investigate his background and training as a teacher of emotionally troubled teenagers, discuss his background as a playwright, his early collaborative books with illustrator Bill Rancitelli, and the unpublished collections, and then concentrate on two of his greatest poetic accomplishments: the Dragon Gate, Inc., books *Narratives from America* (1981) and *A Radiance Like Wind or Water* (1983). These last two books, written while Ronan was struggling to relocate near his "family" of friends and artists in San Francisco, reflect his sense of place and Zen/Catholic aesthetic, demonstrating a new way of writing about love and about the body. Here we find a contemplative, unconventional man accustomed to the tighter spaces of conservative New Jersey but imagining the West as a place of possibility and openness.

II. A CHILDHOOD: PAPER FLOWERS AND PAINTED STONES

> she fell as a child falls
> from its own history . . .
> —Seated Nude,
> *Narratives from America*

Growing up in a two-story row house in Jersey City, New Jersey, Ronan developed a taste for drama and the visual by staging plays with his siblings. Later, he cultivated that taste by visiting New York City to see professional drama. He was born in 1946 to a first-generation Irish immigrant father and a German-American mother. He and his siblings—Louis, three years younger, and Anne Marie, six years younger—grew up in a neighborhood where the neighbors were called aunt and uncle. As the "new family," the Ronans had moved into the close-knit community twelve years earlier. His was a childhood of cultural styles: the family's emotionally evasive Irish side, he later told fellow Irish-American Daniel Healy, played against the unrestricted loudness, zest, and spontaneity of many Italian friends from the neighborhood. (The now-famous drag performer John Kelly, known for his Pyramid Club performance art, also grew up Irish in Jersey City; he was a Ronan friend and model for the cover of his fourth book, *Buddha's Kisses*.)

In one of his childhood pictures, Ronan appears faintly Victorian with his pale features, small hands, and bright trumpet. In another, he is posed next to a magnificently ridiculous elephant on wheels. As a little boy, he used to collect stones and paint them bright colors. Like the names in a Crayola set, these stones promised a colorful transformation of the everyday world into all sorts of cousin objects and other possible lives: fire engine red, caramel yellow, robin's egg blue, lime green. Once dried, these talismans were distributed—at a price—to his neighbors. If, upon opening the screen door of their New Jersey row houses, they did not buy a stone, or if they chose a smaller one over a larger, more expensive one, Ronan would become incensed. He thought everyone should recognize the significance of what he did, that beauty was priceless and worth the nickel or dime it cost for the best red stone.

The Ronan family was loving and close but sometimes complicated for Richard to navigate. In several narrative poems, he unfurls the story of a troubled family whose son is gifted, gay, or in some other fashion unlike anything the rest of them could have anticipated. Otherness, especially an otherness that was partly alleviated by an intense bond between the brother and a sister who's all but his twin, is a particular theme of Ronan's. Responding to life in vastly different ways, the Ronan children shared a complex family love and a common mask: their mother's German-American face.

Ronan's early poetry often concentrates on describing the life and emotions of an introspective man in search of love. The poems about family and childhood do not surface until his 1979 collection, *A Lamp of Small Sorrow*, and then, more evasively in *Narratives from America* (1982). In the later book, the extended poems—each adopting a different persona—seem to speak in symbols from the depths of the self about the author's childhood. These poems, however, are qualified by the introduction's cautious words: "The poems in this collection are not autobiography, or biography." He told his last editor, Gwen Head, that these character sketches were not about his own life. When I asked her which ones she thought might reflect his life, she smiled and said, "All of them."

It is important to note that Ronan believed the relation between a poet's personal life and his writing was debatable, but that real life experiences could give the poetry tones and qualities that make the personal more universal, could change fact into a realistic fable that related one family to many families, and could incorporate other stories into his own, too. His poetic portraits of his family, real or exaggerated, culminate in one of his best and last poems: a bittersweet elegy to his father. In "Poor Flesh," Ronan approaches his father's death with unflinching realism, love, and abandonment. Mysteries and emotions among family, he shows, are not to be unravelled: explanations only draw the knot tighter.

Lucien Stryk, commenting on Ronan's poems about his childhood place and family in *A Lamp of Small Sorrow*, feels that the sequence has an urgent, necessary quality and that "the poet, seemingly lost and overwhelmed in a harsh impoverished landscape, rises above it through meeting it directly, honestly, and with great sensitivity."

After graduating from Holy Name High School in Jersey City, Ronan attended Jersey City State College, a public institution dedicated to training and encouraging creative young teachers. While there, Ronan continued to pursue his drama. He also wrote some poems that would eventually appear in his first book, *Flowers* (1978), and he began developing into a talented and unusual teacher. He graduated from college in 1969.

III. FIRST SKETCHES: THE EARLY COLLABORATIVE BOOKS

In the years before his move west, Ronan taught school and wrote plays. Through the Montclair Public Schools, while teaching emotionally troubled high schoolers, he developed an innovative new program for special needs students at Montclair High School,

9

which was called the Alternate School. He directed and taught at this small experimental program from 1970 to 1985. Ronan employed the full gamut of his interests—poetry, drama, gardening, and Zen Buddhism—to draw out his students. After directing and teaching at the school for fifteen years, near the end of his tenure, he won the Distinguished Teaching Award of Princeton University.

No matter what subject students selected to study, they were apt to be involved somehow in one of Ronan's plays, many of which were staged at the school itself. The roles assigned to these students often served as a subtle form of therapy, relating the individual student's own issues and problems to a "character" he or she could learn to play. Ronan's sister, Anne, designed costumes, and his friends too were drawn into this constant spin of creativity. During these years, Ronan also wrote and directed plays for several New York and New Jersey theatrical companies, including the Riverside Theatre Workshop and the Logos Company. In addition, the poetry he had been writing since college continued to accumulate, inspired by the same vision as the plays.

Many of Ronan's plays read almost like poetry, especially in their stage directions, which hit the opposite pole from Shakespeare's sparse instructions. Because Ronan's drama teems with the stage directions of a very visual man, they read as much like skeletal novels as plays. These directions would be completely lost on the audience, who saw stage directions acted, not read, but Ronan seems intent on the play's reading being as visual as its performance: dialogue alone did not satisfy him. In *Senna*, a play that describes the troubled life of a brilliant, emotionally disturbed woman, a stage direction reveals the writer's controlling eye as much as it does the characters' movements:

> The Father is a slight, intelligent man, capable of internal life but largely inexperienced in much of it. The Mother is a woman on the brink of profound change—she is obviously

burdened: the change has not yet begun. She has a rich and
interesting face. Both are focused on Senna. The Mother
leans against one door. . . . The Father [crosses] thru doors
to B . . . (1)

Ronan's poetry, some of which was written while composing these
plays, eventually comes closer to bridging this gap between the visual and the voiced.

Years earlier, during Ronan's time as a student teacher and before he began the program at Montclair, one of his students had
been a high school senior named Bill Rancitelli. Rancitelli did not
like Ronan at first: "I thought he was way too weird," he recalls
amusedly. But when Ronan began teaching at the Alternate
School, the two men became reacquainted and were instantly best
friends. Rancitelli was a young illustrator—he now freelances and
teaches at the Parsons School of Design—and so it was natural for
Ronan to ask him to illustrate an advertisement for one of his
plays. Delighted by the results, Ronan soon asked Rancitelli to create drawings for a book of poems he was putting together—the
book that became *Flowers* (1978).

Bearing a sample flower or a new poem to be illustrated, Ronan
often would appear at Rancitelli's New York apartment. Many of
the poems were in fact written here. "He was amazed because I
drew exactly what he was thinking, which was the way we worked
together," Rancitelli recalls. Ronan's introspective, serious delicacy
combined with Rancitelli's boisterous, outrageous pleasure in the
world provided fertile artistic ground for both men. They went to
plays and performances several nights a week, traveling around
unreliably in Ronan's conspicuous blue car.

Flowers reads like a homoerotic confessional. Its topics range
from the story of a babysitter fascinated by his young charge, to
the longing a gay man feels for a straight, silent friend. With nods
back to Whitman and Crane, Ronan here uses a common poetic

mode, the love lyric, to extend the range of poetry's expressiveness. Pictures of flowers and nudes, often shown off center in a natural setting, with the fragment of a just-disappearing body or the hook of a bare leg, provide a visual carnival from which the poems spring.

Rancitelli's pictures illustrate Ronan's first four poetry books, collections of words and images that reveal the sensibility of two New Jersey boys—one Irish/German, the other Italian—who grew up eating hot Italian bread, telling fantastic stories, and learning what it was to be gay in the decade after the Stonewall riots but before the first diagnosed cases of AIDS. The poems in the first two books—*Flowers* and *Kindred* (1978)—take risks with content more than they do with form; they strain toward revelation and confession with a voice that sometimes emphasizes uninteresting words or clichéd comparisons. Technical limitations such as these result partly because Ronan had not yet explored the longer, variably lengthed lines that would characterize his best work. The clipped short lines of his early work sometimes substitute terseness for drama. Also, these may derive from his experiments in blending Asian and American aesthetics, a technique he was only beginning to explore in *Kindred* (1978).

Playfully treating desire—spoken and unspoken—between men, these books were targeted almost exclusively towards gay readers. The early poetry is dramatic rather than poetic and was originally conceived for the stage. *Flowers* was written for performance, and Ronan first presented it at The Glines in New York City, and subsequently in Cambridge, Milwaukee, San Francisco, and several other cities. In his sonorous, dramatic voice, Ronan would read, silhouetted by slides of Rancitelli's drawings. The boys in the drawings all look languorous and frozen; their faces rarely show, and they never stare out at the reader. Caught in half-completed action, they depict desire as a process, a motion: just a gentle hand to a sleeping man's neck, or a naked arm leaning quietly to collect crickets, or a knuckled fist proffering a handful of violets to a half-shown lover. The pictures provide a poetry of their own, one of secrecy and private desire. They also give us the fragmented glimpse of reality we perceive when we judge only by what is visible.

By attempting to wed the visual and dramatic, Ronan and Rancitelli created poems and illustrations that form a unique mutual expression of desire. These works, plus his poetic contributions to the magazine *Gay Sunshine*, prompted Gay Sunshine Press editor Winston Leyland to agree to publish Ronan's first real book, *Buddha's Kisses* (1979). At the same time, a small New Mexico press was publishing his first extended experiment in Buddhist/Catholic aesthetics, the limited edition book *A Lamp of Small Sorrow* (1979).

IV. FARTHER REACHES: BUDDHA'S KISSES AND A LAMP OF SMALL SORROW

In *Buddha's Kisses,* themes of desire merge with studies in Asian philosophy to produce a more indirect, complex poetry in which linguistic subtleties are matched by a darker tint of mystery. Ronan incorporates Zen Buddhism into these poems, whose titles reflect this evolving interest: "The History of Kabuki," "At the Vajra Ceremony," "A Lady in the Southern Province," "A Lady in the Eastern Province" (referring to a Chinese custom of relating speakers to their home "province"), and the eponymous "Buddha's Kisses."

Perhaps the most successful of these poems are the two "Lady" poems, whose relationship to two later "Lady" poems can help us chart the impulse of Ronan's western migration. These poems are apparently spoken by Chinese women, but their nationality, like their gender, is left mysteriously unstated. Bowing, perhaps, to the

Asian tradition of masking male actors so they can portray women characters, Ronan's speakers are identified in the title as ladies, but in the poems they seem like feminized men desiring other men. They brood over their desires in loneliness: the lovers have departed, and, exiled from their lovers' bodies and alone with their own desire, the "women" (or gay male speakers) investigate the complex relationship between gender, identity, and desire.

In "Lady from the Eastern Provinces," the absent beloved has left remnants of his masculine body and soldierly duties: shorn hair, fingernails, and blood, and a rusting sword. His "lady" intently stares out her window at a garden that for her embodies masculinity; she projects her desire and perhaps her gender onto the rising phallic landscape. This "landscape projected masculine, full-sized and golden," as Whitman phrases it in *Song of Myself* (647), suggests a suppressed masculinity behind her female mask. Ronan writes:

> the garden has his sword
> rusting in the birdcherry stump,
> the treelets now a foot tall—
> no, this is a lie: they are taller—
> two rising like horns
> from either side of the severed trunk . . . (82)

The remnants and fragments of her lover ironically reveal that the narrator "has" parts of his body but lacks the man himself. The speaker identifies with what is cast out of her lover's body; she subsequently describes the exchange of lust and identity between them. Based on the playful nicknames her love gives his own body—the "maiden's mound" or top lock of pubic hair—he can be identified as being either a man or a woman. In the next strophe, standing alone, two lines center and complicate the speaker's evasive femininity. She says: "I have his seed in the fertile / place: my heart." The indeterminate lover is never finally identified as male or female; the speaker's fertility lies in her—or his—imagination and heart, not in a female womb. The poem's closing lines suggest that, to her, that heart is ultimately a "woman's heart"—and one that is broken. In the final strophe, the narrator says that s/he once:

> stripped the leaves
> from the south willow
> on Loon Pond
> and laid beneath this tree of whips,
> this life of exile,
> daring the autumn now
> to try to try
> to break my woman's heart. (82)

In Chinese poetry, willows and loons traditionally signal romantic—and erotic—love; their conversion into a towering post of whips inverts or expands the concept of eroticism normally found in courtesan poems. The erotic memories conveyed in this poem act as a kind of flagellation for the speaker: just as male and female are blended into one person, pain and pleasure cannot be divided here. But this conversion of willows to whips also imaginatively suggests the pain found in erotic conversions. Changing traditional forms to fit traditionally unacceptable desires may have influenced the poet himself to seek a "life of exile" outside the New Jersey city—and Catholic family—he grew up in. Like the lover in another poem from this book, Ronan's Eastern Lady seems to have the ". . . terrible / sense that any heart that beat / was a heart black with lust, with loss / and one better off not beating at all" ("Buddha's Kisses").

A Lamp of Small Sorrow, printed in limited edition in 1979, is a sequence of four Americanized *fu* poems. Lucien Stryk explains in the introduction that Ronan thought of the *fu* as being close to the American prose poem, but "with a purpose akin to a meditator staring at a single point." It becomes a long narrative form that reads almost like prose, focusing on one natural object, here a back yard, or a city park with an old man crossing it, or a rain-sweating window that looks out on a black lawn and long catalpa pods. Singing with the indirect symbolic weight of each word and object described, this book brings Ronan's personal experience and larger poetic goals to life. The Asian poetic form and the spare photographic descriptions of his New Jersey landscape extend the range of Ronan's earlier poetry, setting the beauty of the changing seasons against the conflict and connectedness of family and vision.

In "Autumn Fu," the upturned, brown bean of the catalpa tree becomes so real the narrator sees both what it is and what it symbolizes for him. From a keenly drawn close description of the plant and dark yard in rain, he takes us into his home, where the parents ominously promise to bury their gay son with them unless he gets married. The mother says, "I guess you can't get away from us." Studying the rotten debris of summer washing up in fall pools, the narrator contemplates this sad confusion of warring realities and realizes:

> the woman is
> terrible in her knowledge of
> loneliness; the man in his denial
> of the same—and I am a little
> like them both.

The poem concludes with its original *fu* meditation on the catalpa pod: hanging phallicly from a leafless tree in a sodden landscape, it falls in water like a knife. And the speaker, crying for himself and echoing the constant rainfall, considers "each thing that comes

16

/ to me, masquerading as a fact, / a pointless truth drawn up / out of the raining world."

A Lamp of Small Sorrow is one of the most honest reflections on urban New Jersey and the conflicts of family yet to be written, but the book is difficult to find and is certainly out of print (as are other books by Ronan; only the Dragon Gate, Inc., and Gay Sunshine Press books are still available through the publishers). Stryk notes that the poems work in the archetypal form of the *fu*, and says that what is remarkable is that "through his very special sensibility [Ronan] has made poems as American in feeling as any written by his contemporaries." What is American is the mood, the collapsing, polluted cities of "gas-tanks that go up and down / like respirators," the "girls . . . all of them androgynous / inside their snowsuits," the old man counting the snails the birds eat, end-lessly rocking on his front porch—a dark, Norman Rockwell fantasy of real things and the mood they infect a young artist with. Through it all, Ronan finds small, believable epiphanies, which are sometimes just the peace of seeing something honestly, and some-times more, as when, in the last poem of the sequence, he sees an old man crossing the highway carrying pussywillows and calls: "goodman, / at last, you have come, / hossanah [sic]." The poet hopes for growth amid the highway of passing trucks, for a vision in the barren landscape, for himself and for others. To use the words Ronan inscribed in blue ink in a presentation copy of the book to his lover, "may all your sorrows be small and useful."

V. SCENES FROM THE INCARNATION

Ronan's childhood Catholicism informs his poetry with an obses-sion for dreams, visions, and a painful sense that the body, which makes incarnation possible, may also keep the soul from heaven. These anxieties and fantasies appear in his later poetry mingled with a Zen Buddhist's sense of life's lovable absurdity and inexorable brevity. But Ronan's Catholic guilt, his fascination with the flesh, and his hunger for visions emerge most fully in his unpublished manuscript written at the Jung Institute in New York City, *Scenes from the Incarnation* (1977). Like Rilke's *Life of Mary* (1913), Ronan's sequence reinterprets myth from the perspective of a fascinated non-practicing Catholic who, as an adult haunted by the church of his youth, now trusts metaphor and language more than religion to interpret and order the mysteries that obsess him.

A self-consciously numbered series of thirteen poems, these long narratives were originally subtitled "a cycle of prose poems." Ronan crossed out those words on the title page, but the excised subtitle suggests that, with these poems, he himself was pondering the question some reviewers asked of his later narrative poetry: Would these pieces work just as well if they were presented as prose?

Ronan wrote that his major emphasis in this collection was on "Christian art as it expressed the drama of the unconscious." His lifelong interest in Jungian psychology appears in other work, more explicitly in his Master's thesis, *Process and Mastery in Basho and Wallace Stevens* (University of California, Berkeley, 1981). Providing a bridge between a Catholic obsession with the body's sins and the soul's difficult salvation, Jung voices some ideas that Ronan later expressed in his own words and works.

Scenes takes the short-lined free verse of Ronan's earlier poetry but fans out from the more focused narrative path of that love poetry. Digressions into visionary experience, such as the Three Kings sighting the star, or the Virgin becoming pregnant by the Holy Spirit, provide the ground for a magical realism that also moves sideways into extended metaphor, lists of adjectives and similes, and other linguistic techniques that suggest ecstatic conversion and transformation. At the end of "The Agony in the Garden," Christ tells the sleeping disciples in Gethsemane that the ultimate terror is not being asleep while he suffers but being aware of his godship, being "awake among sleepers" (9). Telling his disciples the purpose of such knowledge, the speaker plays with metaphor and personification, offering a verbal version of a mystic's vision:

> Why does this happen?
> Oh my dears, perhaps
> so that the moon will gain
> a vein that will ache
> in bad weather;
> perhaps so that its face
> made of canals and dead
> mountains will know pain;
> or just
> that when the chrysanthemums
> unfurl their rust-coloured stars,
> they will be like eyes,
> like mouths, nursing a thorn;
> perhaps so that when the
> world does continue like a herd
> of snails, some of us will know
> its dim secret
> and keep it. (9)

This "secret keeping" is both a religious statement and a poetic one. In *Process and Mastery,* Ronan calls poetry the post-Christian metaphor for living a religious life. The multiple realities available to a visionary prophet and the layered meanings available to a complex poet strike him as being analogous; for both, the truth is simultaneously singular and multiple. A poetic line, like a wisp of smoke in the Jerusalem garden, may be both "the thing itself" and a tunnel or focus for other ideas, feelings, and realities. Ronan argues in *Process and Mastery* that

> such a view does not reduce to meaning. It is meaning, both as transcendental center and manifest periphery. Being is the point: witnessing being is the task; aesthetic comprehension is the meaningful angelic experience. (70)

The angelic experience for Ronan is, in large part, knowing the secret of incarnation. His fascination centers on the word made flesh and, in the poems, on the flesh made word again, rather than on Christ's resurrection. In later poems, the visceral focus on flesh, sexuality, and identity wrought through physical self-awareness becomes even more evident. Here, the visions and digressions always return to insight that makes incarnation, living, more possible.

In an epigraph to *Scenes*, Ronan quotes from the Acts of John:

> . . . Behold thyself in me . . . perceive what I
> do, for thine is this passion of manhood, which
> I am about to suffer . . .
>
> (omissions Ronan's)

This "passion of manhood" expands in the collection to mean both Christ's suffering and that of each man whose life he has touched—shepherd, father, uncle, king. Treatments of Mary and Mary Magdalene movingly recount the story from female perspectives, but the male stories render the Christ story male-centered, underscoring the male camaraderie and eroticism of the collective kings and disciples: the shepherd boy who visits the manger and fantasizes that God is the air in his lungs; the kings who gather toward the light of the star and dream of each other; the "Beloved Disciple" who recalls resting his head inside Christ's shirt, as they slept in snow under an overturned rowboat by the sea; and

Doubting Thomas, said to have seen Christ risen from the grave and not to have believed it to be true, who dedicates his life to the question of his doubt, so fully does he love the man who died.

In the collection's best poem, "Magdalene," Ronan plays with the omniscient voice in an uncanny manner. Ostensibly the story of Christ's reformed prostitute friend, Mary Magdalene, it becomes a sensual portrayal of the unnamed speaker, an indeterminate male voice who may be Christ or even God the Father. He addresses the object of his attention, Mary, as "you":

> The mattress is wet. You turn
> on your side, the knots of matted
> horsehair, like thumbs, under
> your hip . . . . (14)

The scenes leading up to Mary's appearance at Christ's tomb, and her discovery that his body is not behind the great stone door, eroticize the body through this outside, male voice, suggesting both Christ's resurrection (no longer dead, he observes his friend asleep) and Ronan's obsession with the body as instrument of vision and ecstasy. Descriptions of Mary's sexual history serve as a cover story for concerns about the body and the soul's survival past it. Also, as an invocation of Mary through second person voice, the poem shows language's power to create life even when its subject, here Mary, sleeps:

> . . . You've dreamed though
> in fragments. You've a fever.
> The old smells are rising for you
> again: how many of these?
> stale male odors as separate
> and personal as the men who
> opened themselves briefly and
> dripped white here—it's like

> a stairway with them here, the
> ghosts of their flesh rising to
> heaven. (14)

Mary's old lovers, like rising scents, appear through her memory and seem to rise to heaven, but even their ghosts have flesh. As the return of Christ's body is insinuated through metaphor and Mary begins to awaken, a voyeuristic description of her underscores the flesh's part in knowledge:

> You turn over on your back.
> Your breasts flatten like new
> loaves, the nipples red where
> the satin has pulled over them
> against the nape. They are
> heaving with their own thoughts.
> You voyage on the dark smell of
> sweat. . . . (14)

Through a journey to the garden where Christ's body is supposedly interred, Mary passes a landscape more reminiscent of New Jersey than Jerusalem—a feature of many of Ronan's incarnation poems, perhaps signaling his desire for a local manifestation of the miraculous. In this wintry landscape, where "Some of the hedges are glazed with the gritty slush; / leaves look candied," Mary enters the tomb, stops breathing (the narrator instructs her, "stop breathing / let your skin do it instead"), and looks not to find the body here, but to burn a white flame of resurrection. It will light the cave and prove the survival of the flesh from death. Through an accumulation of sensuous detail, the narrative takes Mary deeper and deeper into the cave and the resurrection plot, until she sees Christ is not there and the flame begins:

You can hardly breathe
because of this.
It's first-day: sunday
and the roots of your hair
hurt. There's light in
your lungs. Your breasts
are filling with white
flames and blood. (15)

The body, which Ronan calls a "flammable witness" to our spirits
in a later poem, aches and transforms magically before the signs
of resurrection, as light and blood purify it in a closing image reminiscent of sex and annihilation. The burned, pure body survives
the harmless, burning bush vision of white flame and blood and
once again serves as the site of the joined human and immortal.

In later poems, Ronan further investigates his personal version
of the incarnation, but it is not until his last poem, about losing
his lover to AIDS, that he completely despairs at what this flesh-
bound theory of god means in the face of death.

*

Late in his tenure as director of the Montclair Alternate High
School, Ronan won the Princeton Teaching Award. His empathy
for his students made him an excellent teacher, and it also provided grist for the mind of a constantly creating writer. Several
poems in his fifth collection are dedicated to students whose stories and companionship inspired him.

It was as an extraordinary teacher rather than a poet that he
first came to the attention of one of the editors of the *American
Poetry Review* (*APR*). Editor David Bonanno's former high school
teacher told him of Ronan's teaching work, and the editor was
later pleasantly surprised to receive poems Ronan submitted to
the prestigious poetry magazine. For the rest of Ronan's life, *APR*

played an important part in establishing his reputation as an experimental poet of national import, publishing his poetry and translations seven times in nine years. The editors knew Ronan was a key poet among the increasingly visible gay arts community, and they were intrigued by his work, which reflected a developing interest in combing its author's own life for clues to identity, gender, and desire.

VI. WESTERN MIGRATIONS: SUMMER STAYS AND NEW BEGINNINGS

ronin: *n. Japanese Hist.* A samurai who had for any reason lost his feudal position and strayed away from the barony of his lord; an outcast; an outlaw.

— *Webster's New International Dictionary*, 1934 ed.

For several summers in the late 1970s, Ronan travelled to San Francisco to drink in the foggy climate and enjoy a social scene more accepting of his interests in Zen Buddhism and men. He fell in love with the West Coast in general and with San Francisco in particular. Here he developed a lively family of creative friends who shared a wry humor, an eye for beauty, and a deep love for each other. Much of the remainder of Ronan's life was spent negotiating a move westward toward this atmosphere. This westward inclination and its complicated subtexts are evident in the poetry he wrote during his stays in San Francisco, his year studying at Berkeley, and his temporary moves back to Montclair to fulfill his teaching contract.

Those who knew Ronan believe that California's social openness and its foggy weather and contemplative lifestyle all influenced his love of the place. He was a worrier, a man who wrung his hands frequently and brooded, in a melancholic way, over what could go wrong. The mist and diffused light of San Francisco, which he would later embrace and enhance in the violet-gray diningroom of his apartment on 17th Street, mirrored his introspection, while the bright, frankly happy attitudes of his San Francisco friends warmed him. Most of his friends were more outgoing than he was, but he played the role of the older brother, the ringleader of their tight circle. And for a man seeking some spiritual solace, a man prone to reading Basho in his armchair instead of playing fast and hard in the frenetic gay scene of New York City, San Francisco seemed a peaceful solution. At this time he began to sign his poems, with a Japanese signature stamp in bright red: it said, in *kanji* lettering, *ronin*, a play on his last name, the Japanese symbol for "lawless," one who is outcast from the home barony.

His move west was encouraged by the rapidly growing, close-knit group of friends, many of whom first met each other at Ward Smith's restaurant and art space, named after its location on Russian Hill: Hyde and Green. Mentioned in Armistead Maupin's *Tales of the City*, Hyde and Green was a city gathering place, an architectural marvel carved out of a basement. It served as a magnet for painters, poets, dancers, actors, and others attracted to the constantly changing succession of readings, shows, and performances. Ronan read there; his friend Maz Livingston, a photographer, walked in one day seeking a venue for her antique quilt business; and dancers, actors, and writers often appeared for the performances or just to relax and talk over a cup of coffee. Livingston recalls Ronan's response to the chilly weather and warm social climate of San Francisco in those years: "It was the '70s, it was just so much fun because you could be who you wanted to be, it was the height of that before the sadness came." A talented photographer, she shot Ronan's portrait for most of his book jackets and became his adopted sister and official relationship counsellor.

Ronan was bicoastal for several years before finally ending his New Jersey teaching contract and financing the move west. Most of the years from 1977 until his final relocation west in late 1982 were spent in transit between two states, literally and metaphorically. In his home state, he was a teacher, playwright, brother, and son. In his adopted state, he became an increasingly skillful poet, aspiring ikebana flower arranger, and friend. Hyde and Green remained a central hub of Ronan's West Coast visits, where Ward Smith's friends often were enlisted to staff his larger catering jobs. In the late 1970s, Ronan found himself assigned to pour champagne for wedding guests at a landmark hotel. A new addition, Bill Pittman, appeared at his elbow to help him bartend, and between preparing drinks and flirting, Pittman used his youthful beauty and sense of humor to draw out the sociable but sometimes melancholy poet.

Bill Pittman was a handsome, athletic man studying to be a computer programmer. A committed optimist, he became Richard's great love and temperamental opposite, balancing the brooding introspection of his older friend. Friends describe him as the positive to Ronan's negative, Pittman's way of life a perfect balance to a contemplative, sometimes melancholy lifestyle. With long, curly lashes, light brown hair, and a particular nose, he had, Ronan used to say, a body "like a greyhound": sinewy, muscular, slim. Their connection was instantaneous. When Ronan returned next year to New Jersey to fulfill the last part of his contract with the Montclair School district, Pittman followed him and worked, with a droll, astonished attitude, for the Goody Company, a New Jersey maker of women's hair products. For the rest of their lives, they would be irrepressible and inseparable companions.

*

During the academic year of 1980-1981, Ronan took a leave of absence from the Montclair Alternate High School to study for his

26

Master's in English at the University of California at Berkeley. He received the degree in one year, half the usual time, writing about the poetic process of the Japanese haiku poet Basho and the American poet Wallace Stevens. His thesis, *Process and Mastery in Basho and Wallace Stevens*, mixes Zen aesthetics with Jungian personality analysis, blending a study of traditional haiku with a discussion of the transcendental qualities of the American Modernist Stevens. Just before the year when he moved west to Berkeley, he began searching for a publisher to take on his just-completed manuscript of narrative poems, *Narratives from America*. Studying at Berkeley after fifteen years of successful, innovative teaching was not the only sign of his need for intellectual acknowledgment: he also sought a more mainstream press that could bring his work to a wider audience. One of the best poems from the collection, "Seated Nude," appeared in *American Poetry Review*'s January 1980 issue. This poem caught the attention of Gwen Head, a Southerner who was living in Seattle with her daughter. Head was just beginning her own small press, Dragon Gate, Inc.

When she read "Seated Nude," Head, a poet, teacher, and publisher, was keeping watch for quality manuscripts to inaugurate her press. Instantly interested in the young poet's work, which the author's note said was part of a new manuscript, she contacted *APR* so that she could get in touch with Ronan. Her notes upon first seeing the complete manuscript describe her as feeling "stunned" by the "sheer ambition" and verve of a writer daring "to do a whole collection of dramatic monologues—and get away with the large intentions in these poems more often than not." She noted to herself that

Ronan's best work has tremendous emotional strength and authenticity; he isn't afraid to tackle complex emotional states, expose their pain, illogic and beauty. (Gwen Head, private notes, 16 April 1980)

After a series of careful first letters, the two established a lifelong friendship and an editing relationship that produced *Narratives from America* (1982) and *A Radiance Like Wind or Water* (1984). These books demonstrate Ronan's mature talent. They are stylistically different from one another and from the earlier books. Significantly, they mark his move from smaller, gay-oriented presses to a new but promising press determined to bring its poets to a larger audience. Always eager to earn the attention of a broader audience and more acceptance by American academic poets, Ronan may also have felt his new life in California allowed him the space to write honestly for an audience that included both straight and gay readers.

VII. THE STORY THAT HOUSES US: NARRATIVES FROM AMERICA

And out of what one sees and hears and out
Of what one feels, who could have thought to make
So many selves, so many sensuous worlds ?
—Wallace Stevens
(quoted in *Process and Mastery*)

Narratives from America is a set of sixteen long poems in narrative form, telling the stories of a strange assortment of compassionately rendered, profoundly eccentric characters. *Sipapu* magazine named this the "book of the year" when it was released in 1982. The editors wrote:

. . . the small book that is *Narratives from America* is the closest thing to real American literature that we've seen for many moons. As far as we're concerned, this is it: he's drawn our portrait. (23)

Ronan denied that the poems in the book were "autobiography, or even biography," although Head and others contend that it is largely self-portraiture. Unlike the directly rendered Richard Ronan of his first four collections, the mirrored figure of the author appears here in evasive disguise: he presents himself in the guise of the alienated odd child of "Flower and Stone," refusing to eat anything but increasingly rare flowers, or as the gay brother locked in an attic to cure his "illness" in "The Beekeeper's Sister." A horror of mirrors and the body becomes evident in the story about the Lenapi Indians, "In the Season of the Rutting Moon," and the intense private bond of brother and sister, reflecting his tight bond with his own look-alike sister Anne Marie, appears in four of the sixteen poems. These are family poems that disguise and change the actual family, but which nevertheless remain true to the turmoil Ronan experienced, navigating those complicated waters.

*

Few of Ronan's contemporaries experimented with narrative poetry, and none so successfully. It is not surprising that his interest in drama, his concern about identity in a family, and his evasion of autobiography produced such a daring venture. Upon the publication of *Narratives from America*, Lucien Stryk called Ronan "one of the most experimental of developing poets" and ". . . assuredly one of the very best." He claimed:

> In one of the riskiest of genres Richard Ronan once again demonstrates gifts which have distinguished him among the young poets of today. There is an extraordinary sensitivity and compassion everywhere in this most unusual collection. . . . (back cover, *Narratives*)

An "intensity born of keen listening lives in his *Narratives from America*," wrote Marianne Boruch in the *Small Press Review* (255), who went on to praise Ronan's use of authentic voice in "The

Pickerel," a poem that describes a violently interrupted fishing trip:

> Ronan gives us the thing itself. He knows the boy's voice, what he could think and remember thinking, and keeps tight to that source. (256)

This authenticity stems both from the gothic stories Ronan tells, and from the peculiar voice styles he selected to narrate these tales.

According to Gwen Head, Ronan's poetry owed much to his dramatist's ear, an ear that was attuned more to voice than to music. This voice-ward ear both captures the nuances of human speech and heightens the effect of language by breaking the familiar into tighter rhythms. The human voice's natural ramble retains its original expansiveness—sentences might last four to six lines—but the organizing principle of the poem gathers such language into the artificial unit of the line. Robert Frost said that the American poet should write in the language of Americans speaking, what he called a "sound of sense" that grows spontaneously in everyday speech. Ronan extended Frost's dictum, demonstrating in his range of characters and voices that where there are many voices, there are many Americas. The collective voices and narrators create a texture less consistent than Frost's *North of Boston*, and they show Ronan experimenting with an actor's skill in using voice to reflect the character, the lens through which story and place are viewed.

Where Frost's characters blithely recall a family member who was locked in a cage in an upstairs bedroom, a sort of Yankee Bertha Mason, or they tell of the thinly disguised sexual episodes that turn an elderly judge into a horse gnawing at its hitching post, one of Ronan's characters drags a misshapen body across a garden, listening for the messages of bees; another counts stars silently for days after seeing her reflection for the second time in a long life; a third attempts to kill a beloved sibling by bizarre and creative means; and others stage scenes of personal anxiety and alienation behind stories strange enough to attract tabloid coverage.

The young man in "Flower and Stone" eschews all dietary convention and begins eating nothing but flowers. His strange hungers, which symbolize or suggest other forbidden tastes, worry and finally completely annoy the family:

> We don't know if he subsists
> on a diet of lilies alone,
> but so it seems to us
> as we come to and from the house
> and find him grousing incommunicable
> beneath the privet;
> God knows Brother's odd. (43)

Although this character literally inhales the landscape, truncating spring and frustrating the family minister into calling him a "papist," his strange appetites suggest a screen for homosexuality. His parents worry: "what does this mean? / Where will this lead? Oh, / does this say he'll never marry?" (45).

Alienated from people by his "strange hungers," he devours the flowers with their feminizing, perfumey flavor. Like increasingly exotic lovers, the flowers take him through his "novitiate" of "mere day lilies," through the "wild youth of tulip taking," to his later, wilder, more discreetly secretive days. He eats things the family finds startling and undigestible, things which no one had thought to eat before. They worry as much for their reputation as for his sanity:

> So at last what can we do but sit
> with remnant nerves and some small

> dignity
> and endure the lunatic's legend
> he's wrought for us and himself . . . . (45)

Here, and in the other *Narratives* poem about an outcast gay son (i.e., "The Beekeeper's Sister"), Ronan displays imaginative sympathy not only for his double, the son, but also for the befuddled family. Both poems voice the family's fears and confusion through the outcast's sister. Not only does this narrative strategy increase the effect of alienation (the outcast is another person, outside the central voice), it also engages our sympathies with both the judged and the perplexed judges. And in both poems, a sister ultimately accepts the brother on his own terms. This acceptance may act out personal events, such as Ronan's closeness to his own sister, and it may also be the reward for the cathartic act of giving voice to the voices he perceived to be condemning him.

In "Flower and Stone," the poem's redemptive moment occurs one morning after Brother has deflowered the family azalea bushes. His sister furiously tails him, determined to punish him for ruining her morning and the family's vision of spring. She finds him at the lake, pantlegs rolled up, eating water lilies. She holds the stone she'd planned to hit him with, and then sees his face "transfigured," realizing he is in a Zen-like interaction with the world, in which it is impossible, watching him, to tell the singer from the song:

> It was like I'd imagine a play to be:
> him orderly as a priest,
> moving to a music you would
> hear at church,
> an in-and-out sort of thing,
> the content of the heart turned out
> and worn like a coat; him in the lake,

the lake in his eyes, the heart floating overhead
all white and whiteness. (49)

His speechless joy, the mutual connection between the brother and what he loves, engages her. She becomes part of the picture and, having been infected with his magical vision, she cannot condemn him any longer. She concludes he is a man "of as many sins and failures / as any other, none of them significant / nor unheard of. The same may be said of his / and others' virtues" (50). Reminiscent of Ronan's childhood enterprise of selling tissue paper flowers and painted stones, the sister keeps a stone in her linen drawer after that. She represents the solid things of the earth, he the ethereal visions of sweet-scented flowers. But combined, as in the title of the poem, they create family by sharing two views of a private vision. The stone she had picked up to hit him with becomes a sacred artifact of this vision, a sign of healing and acceptance.

VIII. THE NARRATIVE EXPERIMENT

Echoing his poetic forefather Frost, Ronan opens *Narratives* with an enigmatic, evasive introduction reminiscent of "The Figure a Poem Makes." Ronan wrote this elliptical treatise on self and place in America when he was engaged in the long process of moving to San Francisco, and it reveals some of the tensions of moving from one's place of birth to a chosen home.

"A story houses us," he writes. "Often more utterly than does our flesh." Personality, flesh, house, geography, and country are the outward rippling lines of reality in this collection, and each, he says, is created by the human imagination. Places and events are not meaningful without human interpretation—they matter only as they echo within. This is a theory of reading, whether one reads a poem or a town. It suggests an interdependence between the seer and the seen: "not . . . just the collected wake of events accruing and intersecting into a kind of minor history," he says, "rather the revelation of these events in the realm of conscious meaning." Just as we see not with the eye but through the eye with the mind, Ronan strips back the fiction of pure place, pure experience, and includes the human heart in his equation of reality. "This," he writes, "taken all together, is what I understand as America" (7).

In an earlier draft of the introduction, Ronan glossed the poems' settings, explaining the background of individual pieces, as many poets do before giving a public reading. The original list of names relegated place to mere background detail, but in the revised introduction, place stands beside voice as a central theme and character of the book. As Ronan says, "The voices here, like the times and places, are multiple and operate toward purposes simpler than biography" (7). Set on both coasts and in the American Midwest, as well as in Ireland and Vietnam, the poems particularize experience and offer it in a web of individual voices to demonstrate that place is what one constructs of it. Ronan's own particular fiction of the American West becomes more clear in his next book, since it is largely set in California, but here too he explicitly describes the poetics that made that place meaningful for him:

> I've come to understand this: that one's voice and story, the myth and history of one's country and culture are of a piece—and that if one does not regularly find meaning in some part of this large process, then it is pointless and, at last, hugely dangerous. (8)

The myth of San Francisco, a mecca for gay rights and culture, and the heart of American Zen practice, was drawing Ronan westward as he sent this introduction to his new publisher. Gwen Head met with him in her rambling Victorian house in Port Townsend, Washington, and there, amid walks along the pebble-lined beach of Puget Sound and an antic Dragon Gate, Inc., inaugural party, Ronan's narrative poems took final shape. Eliminating many of his ubiquitous dashes and arranging the poems so that the denser, longer poems did not overwhelm a single section of the collection, Head helped organize the space of the book into a legible pattern, a story house for the voices of Ronan's personae.

*

The *American Poetry Review* poem "Seated Nude" plays a pivotal role in *Narratives* and is one of the boldest pieces in the collection—remarkably so, since its central character is completely fictional. An American woman who is married to a recently paralyzed man, the protagonist takes a walking tour of her husband's native Ireland. As Ronan quested for some deeper sense of home in the West, she too marks an inward journey through a parallel outward one, trying to cure her marital anxieties and escape the horror of this changed marriage. She tries to walk off what cannot be cured by talking with friends:

> . . . the confinement
> to the chair, his death from the torso
> downward, her life tipped over, dragging
> like an oak caught on a leash,
> his embarrassment at being baggage
> to himself, to her . . . . (74)

The woman's attempts to understand her husband's body and the body's place in love make for a remarkably believable and unusual love poem, marked by what Lucien Stryk praised as Ronan's "scrupulous commitment to craft" (*Narratives* back cover).

Toward the close of the poem, the wife locates meaning not in the wet hillsides, but in a dream of her husband at home, seated nude in his wheelchair. Like many Ronan characters, she discovers a solution not in the land or the body, but in an imaginative vision that would not be possible without them. Dreaming of her husband:

> she reviewed his body, his muscled face;
> she knew the man inside.
> His thighs were like stone.
> The absence of his legs was an aching
> in hers.
> She felt the cast fever burn behind his eyes—
> and knew in the most amazing way
> that nothing had changed—nothing: that
> this was their life, unadorned,
> seated in a dream. (80)

The mysterious clarity of a dream enables her to heal herself and reunite with her lover. Love's redeeming and challenging qualities inflect many of the poems in this collection, as does Ronan's evolving sense of place.

IX. A RADIANCE LIKE WIND OR WATER: A POETICS OF THE BODY

> Through me forbidden voices,
> Voices of sexes and lusts, voices veil'd and I remove the veil,
> Voices indecent by me clarified and transfigur'd.
> —Walt Whitman, *Song of Myself*

In the playful spirit of a Buddhist deconstructing gender type-casts, and with the flirtatious seriousness of a man drunk on love and beauty, Ronan casts his fantasies and passions in the delicately figured lyric poetry of *A Radiance Like Wind or Water*. Cousin now more to song than to story, the imaginative lyrics juxtapose the speaker and his lover against natural or domestic objects—moths, dirty dishes, a hollowed sequoia, a steaming bathroom just after the shower. The poetry looks much lighter, freer than that of *Narratives*, partly because its lyric style uses shorter strophes, less regular lineation, and lines that are frequently indented to give the poems a spontaneous shimmering-edged shape. Ronan's words look almost carelessly beautiful. The relationship between the speaker and his obsessions is moderated now by a self-acceptance that was absent in the self-conscious early books and in the distancing, disguised voices of *Narratives*.

The book opens with a series of persona poems, then moves into a more personal voice, vividly detailing everyday life in California in a series of love lyrics about hiking, love making, dish washing, and tea. Demonstrating Ronan's most elegantly simple style, these poems pick up where the first four books left off, telling stories of desire satisfied daily in a committed relationship. Rather than reducing experience to the merely personal, the poems celebrate the Zen appreciation of everyday life: sudsing hands in dish soap, hiking north of Berkeley. And where the earlier poems sometimes strained clumsily at connecting the disparate elements of the beloved, natural setting, and events, these poems leave the reader free to construct a feeling from the juxtaposed objects, people, and situations at hand, to sense the objective correlative at play in the poem. The lyrics in *Radiance* are, as critic Maxine Scates commented, even less controlling than those found in *Narratives*, perhaps because Ronan now more actively involves the reader as a participant in the poem. Like the ikebana flower arrangements he produced in his garage workshop, the poetry places certain elements together in a balanced or tilted arrangement, opening suggestively so that the parts echo and suggest each other, collectively communicating a larger, subtler meaning.

In this poetry, the body is the imaginative site of identity and must be reckoned with carefully. Just as "place" in the introduction to *Narratives* is constructed in the mind of the human witness, "body" in these poems is created by the interpretive viewer, whether he is looking at his own or another's flesh. Reading the body both fascinated and unnerved Ronan, friends say. He was a well-dressed and handsome man, dark haired and bearded with slightly hunched shoulders and a thin body. Yet until his last days, Livingston says, he was insecure about his looks. When he was packing his house and sorting through his belongings during the final days of his illness, she found him terribly distraught over a childhood picture he had found. He told her he had been clearing things from a cupboard and suddenly knew this picture was inside it and was afraid to look. "It had so much sadness connected to it that I just didn't want to look at it," he told her. She recalls that "when he opened the cupboard he just looked in and it was like this person was separate from him, and he said, 'I saw this handsome boy and I realized what I'd done to this boy.'" Teaching himself to be apprehensive about his body, worrying about his body image, had not been entirely quieted by his intellectual self-confidence. The ringleader of his circle of friends, he was shy around strangers and possibly never quite at home in his own body.

Natualizing a gay man's relationship to his body and his sexuality is a key theme of *Radiance*. Its love lyrics take place in the wild or in a home: the lovers embrace in the burnt hollow heart of a giant sequoia tree or hike in the California mountains; elsewhere they lie on their rooftop or stare out the window at birds. These settings testify to the real life romance of Ronan and Pittman and engender a sense that their love, gay love, indeed all love, is both "natural" and boringly, joyously domestic, a homey landscape where, as Ronan writes in "Despair Before Spring," "the daily joins the eye of God."

In "Heartwood," an act of lust in the woods becomes a statement about nature's responsive movements. The nature of the lovers, the interpenetration of bodies and minds, is represented by the hollowed tree that becomes both site and part of the dance. The description of the lovers becomes increasingly busy, and they become difficult to distinguish from the dark trunk they are hiding in—something Ronan shows in image and style, rather than by telling us—and then the speaker finds himself touching the ground, whose own masculine energies and erotic force complement and confirm his own:

> I am sinking my fingers
> into the redwood soot floor,
> touching the place
> from which the root grows down. (10)

He is nature, participating in a wild love in the wild, becoming so entangled with his lover that he cannot tell their bodies apart: "a mouth   maybe mine . . . ." The wild aspect of his love becomes naturalized when the great sequoia itself grows in a parallel motion, symbolizing harmony and endurance past the fires that, as the title suggests, burn the body down to bare heartwood.

Ronan did not make a secret of his homosexuality, either in life or in poetry. Rancitelli recalls that beyond merely being out to his parents, he would in the early years actually bring the unlikeliest boyfriends home to meet them. However the family responded— friends report they were loving, but utterly puzzled—Richard's interest in men was indisputable. What is less clear is how his sexual choice affected his poetry.

As a poet of the post-Stonewall period, Ronan lived at a time when gay culture was becoming more self-consciously unified and publicly visible. Early in the gay press movement, when small presses were beginning to anthologize writings for and about gay Americans, Ronan began publishing his love poems in Winston Leyland's *Gay Sunshine* magazine and in *Gay Roots*, a spin off anthology. Although he published poetry that explored his sexual identity, as an artist Ronan seemed to identify more with the avant garde playwriting circles of New York, partly because there were few venues for gay poets in those days. His poetry's introspective descriptions of desire, flirtation, and passion attempted to contemplate what Rancitelli says others in New York in the 1970s were loudly and unselfconsciously celebrating. In his writing, Ronan was an anomaly and a forefather of many writers who came after him. Leyland calls him one of the ten best poets of the post-Stonewall era.

Although Ronan's early books read like an extended confessional of lust and self-conscious gay identity, he did not work in the few gay writing circles available in New York in the 1970s. Some say he disdained doing what he called the "po' biz" of cafe readings and networking, and until 1984 he did not write explicitly about how homosexuality inflects poetry.

In that year, *American Poetry Review* published a series of Ronan's delicately translated Paul Verlaine poems, along with an introduction he wrote discussing the French poet's background and homosexuality. In the introduction, Ronan instructs readers to look elsewhere for the basics about Verlaine, since they are readily available, but he does pause to discuss Verlaine's relationship with the poet Arthur Rimbaud. Briefly but thoughtfully he reflects on this homoerotic romance and Verlaine's Catholicism, two issues about which Ronan insists the French poet "had feelings."

> The degree to which one's personal life is important to one's work is debatable at best, but what seems clear to me about his love for Rimbaud—or his sexuality, per se—is that it seems to have enriched his poems with special tones and attitudes, stresses, perspectives and tastes that perhaps would never have found their way into language without these experiences and feelings. (23)

40

While Ronan's earliest poetry presents such tones and experiences as powerful surface event, in the *Radiance* poems, form meets content to express a poetics of the body that stems from Ronan's gay experience. He brings flavors and perspectives that are central to his poetry's force and magic and that are new to American poetry itself.

Verlaine, in later life, underwent a fervent attack of religious guilt and retreated into the Catholic mysteries, a decision, Ronan says, that "may have been as real as it was expedient." In this guilt-wracked Neo-Platonism, loving God with an ardor that may have almost matched his love for his young lover, "it seems the divine did come to the man and that it came in the whitened form of the man-child he had loved and suffered for. Perhaps his love at last went where he said it did," to the divine which, as in the poem *Soe*, is found in the mouth of the beloved and in which the beloved is also found.

*

The Japanese term *Soe*, Ronan explains in a poem of that name, means

> the place of man
> in the line from earth to heaven;
> also, the purpose of a man: to be
> the eyes and ears of heaven,
> the blood of earth, the mouth of god . . . (23)

This poem is a celebration of love and looking. It is largely about Ronan's long, intense love for Bill Pittman. Shaking water like a terrier as he leaves the shower, the young man in the poem, addressed intimately as "you," brings to mind gods. The water rivulets coursing down his "tight oiled skin" are celebrated for their distinct sexiness and for their symbolic force, linking the body to the lives of these lovers. The speaker gazes at his damp love and knows:

> . . . our lives
> are running beside each other
> like vines climbing themselves,
> reaching up the bed,
> beneath the breakfast table,
> shared hands/mouth/hair.
> There is a rooted part of us.
> We are an event continuing
> before our own eyes.

Like the roots Ronan reaches for beneath the sequoia in "Heartwood," the radical part of the couple cannot be explained verbally but is just beyond the reach of a set of exquisite metaphors that snake and vine under the table, over the bed. Process and mastery direct the poem and the love, capturing the particular flavors of Ronan's experience with his partner. What may have surprised straight readers unfamiliar with the "flavors" of Ronan's experience is the way in which the love story seems so unusual, put to paper. Simultaneously particular and universal, the poetry describes a romance that achieves Ronan's goal that the truth be both singular and multiple, distinctive to one couple and familiar to anyone who has been in love.

X. JAPANESE AESTHETIC AND CATHOLIC GUILT

Ronan's "Zen Aesthetic" is as persistent in the poetry as it is impossible to describe. Perhaps such an aesthetic is not identifiable through specific style but through content and flavor, qualities that not only surface in the poems but *are* the surface of the poem, much like Ronan's use of gay experience. Haiku poems act as "hinges" to connect the themes and visions of several of the longer

Radiance poems; some also include Zen terms. But the main sense of Zen practice in the poems lies in the poet's close examination of reality and in his underlying belief in life's illusory quality and importance.

Zen Buddhism, which has been present in America at least since D. T. Suzuki arrived in San Francisco in 1897, is more a spiritual practice than an organized religion. Ronan admired Zen's affectionate fascination with life being temporal, simultaneously meaningful and meaningless, and its lack of interest in the closed, reductive European and American ideas of binarism. As a gay man, he embraced Buddhism's distaste for defining all humans as either "he" or "she." As a poet, he revered the great Buddhist poets of China and Japan, whom he had read in translation. As a contemplative person, he admired Zen's quietly transparent engagement with the spiritual aspects of daily life.

Although he perhaps never sat in formal Zen practice, even in San Francisco, Ronan was a serious student of Zen on his own terms. *Radiance* reflects this intent study, partly in that it describes the private life and environment of a Zen practitioner, partly in its themes of life's brevity. Also, its conclusions, sometimes wry, sometimes accepting, are about the holiness of daily life and the permanence of death. Catholicism, which sometimes rings a challenging note in the poems, does not ultimately convince Ronan that the flesh-bound soul can survive. But it remains a force in his imagination, and he relied on his more religious sister to relieve his sense of Catholic guilt, even in the last days of his life.

The tension between Zen and Catholicism plays most fully in the lyric "Despair Before Spring." Contemplating maples and willows of March, this poem's vision extends into a series of interlocking metaphors, literal plants budding with human confusion. The pussy willows and forsythia that reflect "the nude landscape of the soul" are heavy with a Christian vision of spring: resurrection and, just before it, death. Absorbed by the landscape's "unadorned, wild air of saints," the speaker casts back to Zen teaching for insight.

> Says Senno:
> The moment-before,
> not the moment-of
> is perfectest harmony,
> the unopened iris, the just-coloring bud. (29)

This love of the wild, saintly barrenness of desire is met with a Catholic sense of burden, a paraphrase from St. John:

> And the long days, the vast year ungiving
> before the turning,
> says St. John,
> is our fast of abandonment,
> our meaningless endurance. (28)

Faced with one bleak vision and two opposing, authentic-seeming interpretations of it, Ronan's speaker is left "full of hunger, longing / for an alignment with a faith." He turns with more need than resolve to a mysterious symbol of faith itself—one unaligned, as he is, with either prophet's vision: "we try to keep a budded rose / burning in the wet lamp."

Although Ronan had long been intrigued by Japanese flower design and art, he had more access to serious study of such arts on the West Coast. During his San Francisco summers, he had begun studying ikebana, and he even managed to incorporate the great Japanese poet Basho into his UC Berkeley studies in English literature. Ronan's later poems reflect both Basho's simple complexity and the muscular balance of elements in the flower arrangements he designed and sold under the name of "Richard Ronan Designs."

*

Ronan finally moved permanently to San Francisco in late 1982. The poems in *Radiance* reflect how compelling this place was to him—and many were written there. So the theories of American space found in *Narratives'* introduction suddenly gain livelier meaning as his love affair with the northern California coast becomes more established and visible in the poems. In addition to many poems set in San Francisco and the surrounding hills, this new sense of place is signaled in two new "Chinese Ladies" poems, which complete the series Ronan had started five years earlier in *Buddha's Kisses*. Now, subtly different in tone and character, what once was called "A Lady" from the eastern or southern provinces, is now titled "Lady" in a *northern* or *western* province. New Jersey's eastern location disappears under the Asian-California landscape and the Pacific Northwest. And as my emphasis indicates, Ronan's cross-dressed doubles are no longer "from" a place, escaping their home, but are now "in" a place, occupying the West Coast landscapes he loved.

Place poems more directly set in California include "Heartwood," "Egret/Heron/Redwood/Light," "Watching from the Headlands," "Western Autumn," and "A Sighting of Whales." These and other new poems are filled with quiet observation and a poetic voice that locates a sense of home in the Western landscape.

XI. A HEART BLACK WITH LOSS

One of the most unusual poems in *Radiance*, "Poor Flesh," unsentimentally and sweetly eulogizes the poet's father, who died of cancer in November of 1982. Ronan began drafting the poem in New Jersey, where he was staying during the final months of his father's life. At this time, he was commuting to a hospital room to sit in shifts, with his siblings and mother, by the bedside of the cancer-stricken man. Maxine Scates, writing in *Poetry Northwest*, praised this poem in which "the world is chaotic, and the poet's

45

quest for meaning takes on added poignancy." The quiet technical achievement of *Radiance* pleased her here and in other poems, "often unnervingly quiet in their composition," as "we hear language relaxing into questioning and longing" (127). *Sipapu* magazine attributed the realism and emotional honesty in "Poor Flesh" to the increasing Asian influence on Ronan:

> His study of Zen and Japanese culture has led him not to obvious borrowings of their trappings, but to a harder look at the colors of his own northwestern world; exact descriptions of koi and their colors, or the wooden taste of Japanese tea, become even stronger when applied to his father's long dying . . . . (34)

"Poor Flesh" is a series of collaged impressions, both contemplative and harshly honest. These logically extend the meditative wisdom of Ronan's *Lamp* poems, in the same kind of personal narrative. But here, the most honest and emotionally jarring truth comes when close observation does not lead to insight. The speaker cannot see past death or even loss.

Set both in the hospital room and on the highway between the hospital and Ronan's apartment, the poem chronicles several kinds of journeys that take place during the family's bedside wait. Jazz-like in its blocks of raw sound, placed without transition or explanation beside each other in a song, the poem puts pain killer solutions (MORPHINE SULFATE / IN SODIUM SOLUTION/ 500 CC) next to weird visions ("In his body my father's soul is burning, / as if the body were a smooth thin tree") next to memory and the ever-present, inhuman landscape Ronan turns to for solace and understanding. The poem has many potently lovely passages, offering a message that we must live and bear witness to both life and death.

On one of his drives to the hospital, Ronan prays that God let him see the pattern of life and death as beautiful; he finally describes his father's death in the third person: his brother alone was with their father when he died. Louis Ronan, whose own horrified near-death experiences in the Vietnam War are recounted throughout the poem, holds his father's hand as he dies. Ronan later describes this scene clearly as if he were there, imagining his father's concern for his brothers

> . . . lest you be as frightened as he was,
> alone in the jungle, drugged,
> in horror, watching the anaconda hatch its young
> in his shoes, his heart.
>
> You open your eyes.
> He wakens and takes your hand.
> Your eyes are no longer glazed gray, but clear,
> perfected.
> You do not speak, but seem amazed,
> yourself again and profoundly calm.
> He holds your hand. You are alone together.
> It is very quiet in the flickering light.
> When you die, you do so gently
> so that it does not frighten him. (53)

The act of presence and community is the family's and the poem's terrible responsibility and only hope. Process counts as the ultimate reward: if there is afterlife, for Ronan it seems to be in the memory of one's loved ones. Life itself, including the experience of dignified dying, is the crucial way through the mysterious questions that alternately puzzle and frighten this narrator and his family:

We do not know what to say,
but know that we must witness it,
that we must witness each other,
that this will make enormous difference. (53)

*

Many of the poems in *A Radiance Like Wind or Water* began on
long legal pads in the violet gray diningroom of Ronan's 17th
Street flat in San Francisco, where filtered light from the
Japanese garden outside played against the wall. There he com-
posed poems that provide not only a Zen meditation on life's tran-
sience but also a Catholic morbidity about the body. The poems
would then be transferred to an electric typewriter. Although he
lived for eight years with a computer programmer and always had
a word processor in the house, Ronan prided himself on his complete computer illiteracy. Typing in the white-walled office near
the front of the house, he would revise the poem. Final or nearly
final versions would be sent to Head, often in bundles in which
each poem was stamped by his red-inked Japanese signature
Ronan.

XII. LAST SEEDS: THE FINAL YEARS IN SAN FRANCISCO

I have his seed in the fertile
place: my heart. . . .
"A Lady in the Eastern Provinces," *Buddha's Kisses*

Ronan lived in San Francisco permanently from late 1982 until
his death in 1989. His ikebana business, "Richard Ronan Designs,"
thrived for several years, as he acquired major clients, including
Singapore Airlines, Wilkes Bashford, and several Knob Hill families. He would drive to Sonoma County to scout for rare strains of
bamboo, and he would root corkscrew willow from the arrangements to plant in his friends' gardens. Dried lavender hung in his

garage workshop, where he clipped and selected flowers to go in the wire frogs and clustered pebbles of the ikebana vases. He had trained in the Sogetsu school of flower arrangement, which stresses creating innovative designs from the classic three elements: heaven, earth, and the world below are represented by the flowers, arranged in a triangle. Muscular, precise, and unusual, his floral arrangements, like his poetry, teased new inflections out of traditional themes.

The dining room where Ronan wrote most of his San Francisco poems looks out onto what was once a small backyard, a "stubby little city garden," his friend Marlene Blessing says, that he transformed until it was "dripping with shapes and colors." This tiered Japanese garden in the Upper Haight grew and gained its own green voice outside the diningroom window, filling with rooted plants from the ikebana arrangements and with other rare botanicals Ronan had collected and nursed. Its shaded slopes play with light and angled lines in surprising ways, as the bright lime of a Norfolk pine's fisted whorls give way to a low leafy ceiling of flowering maple, red blooms resting on a slatted archway. The saplings of this garden are pruned for a crosshatched ascension to the San Francisco sky, and numerous varieties of fern, ivy, and bamboo rise and fall in shaded beds behind a Japanese lantern and a stone-ridged goldfish pond. Against one wall, a miniature temple stores the Buddhas on a ledge, where they can watch and bless the shifting greens and stippled flecks of light that winnow through the garden's leaves. At the base of the garden, where a red sign spells out Ronan in Chinese lettering, the diningroom window and a converted mud-porch spill onto a patio lined with orchids. Plaster and terra cotta angels are nailed and hung on the side of the house and the garden wall. This small but lovely property, originally rented, was later purchased by Ronan and Pittman.

During the last years of Ronan's life, this garden became the central expression of his aesthetic, a space for combining the California dream with a Japanese philosophy of design. The sunfaded Adirondack chairs by the *koi* pool, the small table on the concrete porch below the rise of roses and flowering trees, became a living poetry in which he could find some peace when he was too tired, too sad, or too ill to write.

Ronan and Pittman's house also reflected a California-Japanese aesthetic. The long, lean apartment took on an understated elegance, with antique Japanese prints, scrolls, and *kanji* script gracing the hallway. Unusual vases, some designed by Pittman, appeared—a different one for every occasion—bearing Ronan's ikebana, which rose with graceful athleticism from the water. Despite the apartment's usually sophisticated style, the two men had a special place for shameless kitsch. Plastic sushi was their specialty.

They had travelled to Japan twice; on one of these visits, they relentlessly hunted down the elusive quarter in which plastic-food craftsmen were clustered together with fellow members of their guild. The lovers' prize, an arrangement of disturbingly authentic looking shrimp and grated daikon, rested in their home on a pottery dish that, on closer inspection, also turned out to be plastic. It was, as Head reflects, "Buddhist sensibility meets plastic kitsch." In the delicately arranged apartment, such anomalies nodded toward the wry humor Ronan inflicted on his friends: three-dimensional religious postcards, monstrously ugly 1950s lamps, and other design elements that threw his spare Zen style into relief.

The house was a center for the close circle of friends who celebrated "family holidays" in style. This loyal and imaginative group was local and bi-coastal, as friends from New York regularly visited. Lovingly hosting the Italian mother of his old friend Bill Rancitelli, Ronan spent one day driving to dozens of Italian delicatessens in San Francisco, searching for the exact ingredients she required to make a big dinner for the men she treated like adopted sons.

In 1985, Pittman was suffering from frequent colds and sudden weight loss. He was diagnosed HIV positive; thereafter Ronan's life centered on attending to his sick lover. Their friends rallied and took turns sitting at Pittman's bedside and keeping him company during tests and treatments. For Ronan, who was later diagnosed himself, staying strong for his lover and fighting against his own illness and depression became too much for him to continue writing poetry. For the next two years, he lobbied aggressively to get Pittman onto drug trials (he was one of the first people to take the then experimental drug AZT, which was originally given at very high dosages), while helping him with his chosen routine of healthy home remedies. Visualization, a careful diet, exercise, and a teetotaller's avoidance of alcohol were all part of Pittman's routine. Ronan was as gloomy about their disease as Pittman was forcefully positive. The only published poem about this time in their lives, "Love Among Lepers," appeared in *American Poetry Review* four months after Ronan's death.

This unflinchingly honest poem has the ache and depth of a symphony, but it addresses death and loss in an unsentimental style—a task Ronan had earlier accomplished in his elegy to his father. Through a lens of hard-eyed realism, the poem magnifies the speaker's enormous sense of loss, addressing the impossible pain of seeing Bill die and the impossibility of not watching. The speaker reveals that this is not only love of a dying man—it is written by one too, his lover "among lepers." First, when the speaker describes his lover losing his body, he uses the leprosy metaphor literally:

> if he has, since last loved, lost a lip
> & is now imperfect of any answer, even to our softest, sweet
>   word . . . (24)

Writing about a leper and then about body-loss in a more abstract
sense, Ronan circles around AIDS—and any terrible disease—by
examining his lover's pain, his own sense of loss, and the profound
confusion of nursing someone who is suffering from an affliction
identical with his own. As the poem's central metaphor evaporates
with the leper's body, leprosy becomes at once more personal and
less real, a description of any body lost to any disease or sorrow.

In earlier poems, Ronan spoke of the body, specifically, of the
male body, as the place of God. But in this poem, such conviction
makes the lover's death especially disastrous, as the speaker
keenly mourns the loss of "that which was divine, that to which
you gave flesh . . . ." The abstract gropings, in earlier poems, for a
way to express his fascination with the fleshy, earthbound end of
incarnation, become hard and sad and real as Ronan writes:

> Beloved, I love you & there is no god.
> Oh, I love you and there is no hope.
> Look how we are still so hungry for each other
> & still we will not live. (24)

This poem rants against a poetics of witnessing, in an angry,
hard-edged version of the elegiac vision of "Poor Flesh." Here the
furious and passionate speaker protests death even as he struggles
for words to describe its literal face and the emotional impression
it makes upon him. The poem's paradoxical honesty lies in its
seeming contradictions: Ronan witnesses even his own ambiva-
lence to witnessing, talks about his speechlessness before his
lover's death. In the end, this compulsive and beautifully rendered
vision of his own pain blooms into loving and self-resentful poetry,
as the speaker closes his half-aware lover's eyes to blank out his

dulled vision, and wonders, in the last line, "why it is we live to see such as this again?"

*

In the winter of 1986, Ronan and Pittman travelled disastrously, romantically, to London on a surprise trip Ronan had planned for them. At the British Museum, he leaned uncomfortably against a slag of stone and contemplated the ridiculous, failed journey, regretting dragging his ill lover across the ocean for a vacation he could barely enjoy. Then Ronan realized he was leaning on the Rosetta Stone. Later, he told several friends about a visionary moment, in which—he told Livingston—ripples moved across the ancient, cryptic stone, marking time and space so visibly that he could imagine the movement, like water, crossing history and bringing together the rippling lines until they collected around the Americas' East Coast and Japan, to end on the West Coast of America, in San Francisco. Head recalls that, in the version she heard, this map of time and the world was crossed by a fiery root tip, like a finger, tracing in an instant a passage across time and space. In his vision, as Head wrote, "this westward-moving force of human history now stood poised on the Pacific rim, facing an equal force that had gnawed and burrowed its way with like intensity through the ages and countries of the East . . . " (Gwen Head, personal diary, 3 June 1988).

Pittman was walking toward him as he shook out of his trance, and he clearly heard a voice tell him, "And that's what this disease is about, you see."

His friends and lover, caught and moved in the moving lines, and his fascination with the Pacific Rim and San Francisco's contemplative lifestyle, all shimmered in his vision toward the West Coast location where they met. He said later that they were all meant to meet, that the Japanese and American aesthetics were meant to join in California; a new force was rising from the ruins

53

of disease and sorrow, from the meeting of American and Asian culture. The interpretive stone, an enigmatic key to biblical and ancient languages, became a private sign he didn't understand but felt compelled to share. It may have been his strangest poem.

During the last weeks of his life, Ronan had Livingston photograph his garden so that she and Healy would know how he wanted it kept when they inherited the house. Livingston reflects: "We didn't talk about it but as we looked at the photographs what we thought was gardens change, and he was doing this to preserve it exactly the way it was and we realized that we couldn't, that life goes on and it changes." The violet-gray diningroom, where his writing took place, now glows in layered shades of Monet yellow, transformed by the new tenants, who have lived there for several years now. They won out over other prospective renters when they mentioned they wanted to work on a Japanese garden, apparently unaware that one covered three levels behind the house. Still bearing Ronan's *"ronin"* sign in Chinese lettering on a low wall, the garden is a shaded, meditative forest of ferns and bamboo, startling in its pruned shapes and sudden colors. In mood and design, it is much as Ronan created it: rosemary and ivy frame the *koi* pond. Crossing the stone steps of the second tier, you smell creeping mint underfoot, see violets by the low lantern.

One of the strange changes is the ghost in the basement. A few years ago, the new tenant, John MacGregor, called Healy to ask some questions about the former tenant. Had he worn an old blue workshirt when he gardened? Did he have wire rim glasses, a scraggly red beard?

Healy answered: "Yes. Why?"

MacGregor said, "We've seen him."

MacGregor's son had been in the dusty basement garage, a cavernous cement space as large as the apartment above it, when he saw a figure next to the washing machine. This lightless cement room, where boxes and tools lay piled on shelves and on a great wooden work table, was Ronan's ikebana flower studio.

His friends speculate that Ronan returned for the tea house. He was, after all, a perfectionist, and his garden is in transition. After a wall was damaged by a fallen tree, the tenants asked Healy if they could replace part of the barrier with a Japanese tea house. This serendipitous event, emerging from the disaster of a felled wall, would have pleased Ronan, or *dis*pleased him, perhaps, if its construction were stalled. He had always wanted to build a tea house in the garden himself. So rumors of this meticulous man pacing through the house strike his friends as being uncanny but predictable: "He's probably walking down the hallway wringing his hands saying, 'Where's my tea house? You promised me a tea house—'" Livingston says, frowning in impersonation of his seriousness, and then laughing.

*

Bill Pittman died in 1985, just before Thanksgiving, two years before Ronan himself died from advanced complications of AIDS. The last poem Ronan is known to have written describes the circle of friends who gathered the day after Bill's death for a modified, defiantly loving Thanksgiving feast. Two years later, Ronan died from advanced stages of AIDS and also, his friends say, from a broken heart. His last years had been lonely ones, even with the rallying circle of friends, a remarkable home hospice worker named Eric Poché, and the support of his sister, Anne Frey. On 7 November 1989, surrounded by many of the people he loved, Ronan died.

His last poem reconciles mourning and autumn with spring and Easter. It describes the friends who helped and attended the men, gathered for a difficult Thanksgiving the day after Pittman died. Ronan sent hand-signed copies to friends as a gift his last Easter. In the poem, the ripe holiday table is set with friends, not food, and the poem burns with the fleeting beauty of these companions who witnessed his saddest day, drawn together to consume but at the same time to remember something sacred among them:

> We sit in the garden
> at the center of the heart,
> watching the wheel turn,
> smiling, a moment or two after terror,
> past the dark loss, the mad ticking mystery,
> our own centers flinging apart — plates laid out
> briefly on a table suddenly orbiting the sun.

> Praise be to the table, spilling its array.

> May God abide in the plate
> ladened to overflowing.

> Oh, that we can so love one another
> in this place.

XIII. RICHARD RONAN AND THE AMERICAN WEST

Some might speculate that because he was a resident of the American West so briefly, Richard Ronan barely had time to absorb its literary and spatial influences or to leave his own mark. But much of the sense of place in the later poetry and the sense of movement from the poetry of the late 1970s on owes an emormous debt to Ronan's almost mystical belief in what the West could represent for himself as an Eastern-born, westward-moving poet. His relation to the West is a poet's double love of the real and the imaginary. As a writer, he is devoted to the space where he could pursue his meditative interests in ikebana, Zen, and poetry.

Ronan was influenced by the example and lives of other poets and artists who inhabited California as a place of imaginative possibility. For many of the writers it also proved fertile ground as they invented themselves likewise as hybrids of East and West, scions of Basho and Wallace Stevens. Here, Gary Snyder, Kenneth Rexroth, Alan Ginsberg, and other San Francisco Renaissance writers created themselves as America's own version of the Buddhist poet, laughing too loudly and scaring away curious tourists who too gravely approached the temple. Ronan follows in the spirit, if not precisely the poetry, of these poetic forebears. He shares their interests and enormously independent style, more than he sounds their notes or speaks as their echo.

As one of the few American poets of his age to experiment extensively with the narrative form, Ronan had few poetic equals or ancestors. Whitman comes closest, an influence for the long lines and the erotic openness of the poems. Whitman also urged artistic descendants such as Ronan to voice their age and in some sense create it through that voice. Other prominent gay poets served as examples and exemplars—Verlaine, whom he translated, comes to mind—but Richard Ronan was in many ways a true American original.

Scanning his East Coast background for clues leaves one with chalky fingers and the smell of stage makeup—but no clear answers. Ronan's teaching and experimental theater were important to his poetic development, as fellow Dragon Gate, Inc., poets often have observed. His line sprang from voice and vision, where theirs often came from music. But the plays are artistically much less distinctive than the narrative and lyrical poetry, and writing plays may have trained his ear and eye away from theater and into imagistic voice poetry more than it proved an easy continuum into the poetry. Playwriting trained him, but poetry was his instrument.

Ronan is a poet who wrote himself into the story of the West. Indeed, his work seems not directly influenced by key West Coast writers, and it has not been widely anthologized. Gwen Head and others, however, know he is a poet's poet—someone who has been read more by other poets than by general readers. His gay press books and their devoted following, and his connection to fellow Dragon Gate, Inc., poet Laura Jensen and to poet Sandra McPherson are certainly subtle but important connections. But Ronan's work, with its egrets and redwood filtering light, casts the West as an imaginary space filled with longing and real with secrets, and it creates himself as a unique man and a parable of the open space he chose to write about and inhabit: a large, wild, new State, blank enough to serve as the setting for every variety of hybrid and self-invention. The West figures as a central figure for Richard Ronan's inspiration and self-invention, and in that sense, he is a grandson of Walt Whitman, singing not only America but its western fringe, and singing not only the real place but the longing for what it represented and could allow him to be.

Selected Bibliography

Archive of manuscripts and unpublished material: much of Ronan's work is currently housed with his last publisher, Gwen Head, in care of Dragon Gate, Inc., 508 Lincoln Street, Port Townsend, WA 98368.

PRIMARY SOURCES

Ronan, Richard. *Buddha's Kisses*. Bill Rancitelli, illustrator. San Francisco: Gay Sunshine Press, 1980.

———. *Flowers*. Bill Rancitelli, illustrator. Ithaca, NY: Calamus Books, 1978.

———. *Kindred*. Bill Rancitelli, illustrator. Buffalo: Audit Press, 1978.

———. *A Lamp of Small Sorrow: Four Fu Poems*. Bill Rancitelli, illustrator. Laguna, NM: A Press, 1979.

———. *Narratives from America*. Port Townsend: Dragon Gate, Inc., 1982.

———. *A Radiance Like Wind or Water*. Port Townsend: Dragon Gate, Inc., 1984.

———. "Clover," "Sexton," and "Sweet Cherry," in *The Son of the Male Muse* (gay poetry anthology). Ed. Ian Young. Trumansburg, NY: The Crossing Press, 1983: 154-62.

Verlaine, Paul. "Thirteen Poems Translated By Richard Ronan." *American Poetry Review* 16 (July/August 1987): 23-26.

UNPUBLISHED MANUSCRIPTS

———. *Haiku Versions*. (poetry) Montclair, NJ: 1982.

———. *Process and Mastery in Basho and Wallace Stevens.* M.A. Thesis, University of California, Berkeley, 1981.

———. *Provincetown Pieces.* (unpublished prose poetry 1975).

———. *Scenes from the Incarnation.* (poetry) NY: The Jung Institute, 1977.

PLAYS

Ronan, Richard. *Antigone.* (Unpublished) New Jersey: 1976.

———. *Cakes.* (Unpublished) One act drama in French and English.

———. *Cakes and Ale.* (Unpublished) Two-act comedy he called a "vaudeville for three actors." A now-lost soundtrack was available for those producing the play, according to Ronan's listing in *Gay Theatre Alliance*'s 1980 directory.

———. *Cecily's Gala, or Sins of the Father.* (Unpublished) A "one-act expressionist farce on morality and roles."

———. *The Chosen.* (Unpublished) A one-act drama. Ronan's synopsis in *Gay Theatre Alliance*'s directory describes it as "a minimalist/expressionist play, obliquely involving a near-catatonic boy and an older man and the former's self-inflicted religious drive."

———. *Hippolytes.* New Jersey: 1976. (Unpublished) A two-act drama blending Greek myth with Oriental thought.

———. *Medea. Poets' Theatre: A Collection of Recent Works.* NY: Ailanthus Press, 1981: 60-69.

———. *Senna.* (Unpublished) New Jersey: 1977

SECONDARY SOURCES

Articles and Reviews

Boruch, Marianne. "Below Ground: Small Press Review." *Iowa Review* Spring 1984: 251-65.

Helbing, Terry, ed. *Gay Theatre Alliance Directory of Gay Plays.* NY: JH Press, 1980.

Scates, Maxine. *Northwest Review.* 23.3 (1985): 124-28.

Sipapu Magazine. 13.1 (1982): 23-24.

———. 15.1 (1984): 34.

Poetry About Ronan

Head, Gwen. *Three Poems for Richard Ronan.* Includes the poems "Night Sweats," "Home Care," and "Ladies of the Farthest Province." *American Poetry Review* 19.6 (November/December 1990).

Personal Interviews

Much biographical material for this book was culled from interviews with Marlene Blessing, David Bonanno, Anne (Ronan) Frey, Gwen Head, Daniel Healy, Winston Leyland, Maz Livingston, John MacGregor, and Bill Rancitelli. Their descriptions, memories, and suggestions were an invaluable resource, without which retelling Richard Ronan's story—flawed and subjective as any biography is apt to be—would have been impossible. To each of them, and especially the extraordinarily generous and intelligent Gwen, my deepest thanks.